LOVING THE
ALIEN

For Ian,
whose love always brings me (gratefully)
back to earth

LOVING THE
ALIEN

by
LAURIE KRUK

Your Scrivener Press

Library and Archives Canada Cataloguing in Publication

Kruk, Laurie, 1962-
    Loving the alien / Laurie Kruk.

Poems.
ISBN 1-896350-20-8

    I. Title.
PS8571.R788L68 2006   C811'.54   C2006-905268-9

Book design: Laurence Steven
Cover design: Chris Evans
Cover photos: courtesy of Laurie, Mark and Betty Kruk, and Ian McCulloch

Published by *Your Scrivener Press*
465 Loach's Road,
Sudbury, Ontario, Canada, P3E 2R2
info@yourscrivenerpress.com
www.yourscrivenerpress.com

Canada Council   Conseil des Arts
for the Arts   du Canada

We acknowledge the support of the Canada Council for the Arts
which last year invested $20.0 million in writing and publishing throughout Canada.

Nous remercions de son soutien le Conseil des Arts du Canada,
qui a investi 20,0 millions de dollars l'an dernier dans les lettres et l'édition à travers le Canada.

Acknowledgements:

I would like to thank Laurence Steven for his keen editing acumen and his commitment to Canadian publishing.

I would like to thank my parents for passing on a passion for reading books, talking about books and even writing books–and for their wise understanding.

And I would like to thank my mate, our children and the ever-widening circle of family, friends and community members that embraces me here. You have all inspired, challenged and sustained me as a writer in my new Northern home.

I would also like to thank the following publications, where some of these poems have appeared:

Somewhere Across the Border: An Interactive Poetry Magazine, Canadian Literature, Springfever–[W]rites of Spring 1997: An Anthology of Poems from the Ontario Division of the League of Canadian Poets (Your Scrivener Press) and *Licking Honey Off a Thorn–[W]rites of Spring 1998: An Anthology of Poems from the Ontario Division of the League of Canadian Poets* (Catchfire Press), *Rampike, Grain, The Fiddlehead, Northern Prospects* (Your Scrivener Press, 1998), *Journal of the Association for Research on Mothering.*

"Believing the strangest things,
Loving the alien..."
—David Bowie, "Loving the Alien," Tonight
(1984)

Table of Contents

Loving the Alien

Vaudevillians of Time

Iceberg Rider

When Her Thighs Were Perfect

Personal Effects

The Mother Robe

About the Author

LOVING THE
ALIEN

Crazy Glue

different worlds. won't
work. he can't keep a job. two kids.
custody battle! god. his ex—
wonder if she's pretty, if she's good
in bed—winds herself around him,
moans loudly, sleeps
soundly?

sleeping together
the first time,
should be clean and white
as the feather duvet
you threw over me
like a handful of snow
instead—
you're hot as a pistol, you say
and yawning, float away,
turning drifts
into waves

* * *

awake, awake
my engine heart
humming, dangerous,
keeps mind chasing
howlings of red
spilling from your window,
old fridge's mutterings
towards mechanical
climax

deep in dreaming–look:
how his mouth sags, heavy
with breath. his skin,
how it fits him.
why can't I follow,
for once? stubborn-shy dancer,
refusing to be led.

* * *

three fridge cycles later,
patches of dream
tape together the waking
till tiny explosions
(birdsong)
unglue my lids.

Up
early: new job, you are
climbing lightly
over a warm obstacle. I harness
my breathing
to your steps, your breakfast. No exit
will ever be so gentle. You leave
an egg-stained plate, the second key,
me in bed
(The Woman, Asleep)

lock turned
from the other side.

Jumping out of bed, I am stuck

in damp shadows of the sheets,
song of the fridge,
fingerprints–
in the grooves of an l p
(David Bowie), still cued

hooking me.

Underwear on backwards, hurry out
before my footsteps harden. Key
shining
on the table.

But, like a broken record, all
morning, all day, all
week
something sticks, bumps
and repeats,
keeping me   stuck.
Something

will not let go
until it takes its piece of me.

7 Days
of Looking at a Single Rose

Monday
Exciting crackle
of cellophane package
squeaking out shyness, he hands
it to me
outside the bedroom. Something
I am reluctant
to unwrap
beneath blue heat
of his gaze.

Tuesday
The proud height of a rose
enthroned
on my kitchen table.
Lords it
above teacup, newspaper:

proclamation!

Wednesday
A touch
brings the discovery:
they breed them
without thorns now;
stalks smooth and safe
for even the rashest
hand.

Thursday
The immodest pink
of it

as outer petals begin to spread:
a pink
that catches me
on my way through the kitchen

ruling
the atmosphere, bringing
an increase of pressure.

Friday
When I bend my face closer
to sip: musical sweetness
singing me near

this single
pleasure. One
to be shared.

Saturday (morning)
I call him. Wearing
yesterday's graces,
the rose
is an exhausted dancer.

you can stay
at my place   *tonight*

put down the phone, touch
a petal
    it
        falls, heavenly
spent.

Sunday (evening)
Doing two days' dishes in a crash
of soapy water, I tidy up

fold the softening stem,
wind-broken umbrella. Nest it
in newsprint.
Crimsoning tissues escape,
spot the linoleum:

tears, bleeding
from a grateful
smile.

English as a Second Language

The cappuccino-sticky table shakes,
as he passes me a folded yellow paper.
Foolscap, we used to call it,
when I used it in grade six. Six short sentences
tightly-knotted,
like a pre-schooler's shoes.
Shakespeare's sonnets
crumble into dust
as I look on my memorial:

*"luv. i wont to tel you how I fil abut you. you are
pachinit an intins. I injoy our cunversations verry
much."*

—nervous skip to the end—

"am proud to cal you my gerl."

I am blinded by
his eager blue headlights, waiting.
I am the Ph.D.,
he is the one comfortable
in his words.

"See, I like to write, too.
Wanted to put it all down, my feelings, on paper.
Someday, gonna do the story
of my life. But first, gotta learn
to write better. Thought you could help."
Sits back, sending the table shaking,
hands curled like question marks.

Pushing aside my stammering blush, cappuccino cup
I pick up a pen. Sigh,
and start, "Okay: if you mean it. First, your spelling needs work.

For instance, you need another 'o' here—"

Circle confidently, then pause to re-read:

"you are a god companun"

Different Worlds

Driving from Vancouver to Whitehorse
and back
he relied upon an eight
-tenths empty
toothpaste tube.

I bought a new one,
specially. Each time I brought it out,
generously-oozing cylinder of peppermint,
he dug into the glove box
for his flattened tongue of plastic
and scrapings of Colgate.
There's enough here, for me. Save yours.

the children of her men

join her in tunnelling a race
to the heart of his heart. Roommates, friends, and lovers
have all come trailing these rivals. Declaring war,
both sides exchange ages and steal tricks—
the puffed adult lip,
sulking over the juice cup
when Daddy and new Girlfriend
touch outside the bedroom
("Do you love her *again*?");
the lipsticked clowning for a kiss, making him late
on his rush out the door
to pick them up from his Ex,
now gnawing on her polish.
Jealous tantrums at five
become PMS at thirty. Tensions hidden
behind too-cute gifts, crayoned portraits of orange-haired women
("Is that me?" "Nope. My real mummy, the pretty one.").
Sizing up the opposition,
now cunningly small, now boomingly tall
they fight, fiercely smiling,
for the very centre
of the Kodak moment.

* * *

yet, cut her in two:
the beloved
and the (other) mother

on the camping weekend,
strangers see only
that she touches them gently
calls their names lightly.
Like Mary, fills the gap
in the family photograph;
hands, hovering like haloes,

uncover a welcome servitude.

First morning in the tent, before they wake,
he taps her belly, says
"Still wonder when you're gonna put something here."
Calls it a joke.
She wrenches away, hipbones knifing.
It would take an act of God
–thank God–since the operation he had
to please his (now-ex) wife.

Then, five years old again,
she sees him
tenderly minister,
as he traps them in nightgowns, first night
trustingly whole-skinned.
Next evening, the older
wants to play "Show me," giggling
and shrieking and flipping up her gown.
"We don't do that, it's not nice."
And helps
the younger to pee
lifting her up, half-naked
on the trail of the campground
while she frowns, glancing at the next tent.
"It's only a kid."

Next day, she's changing for swimming;
he catches her shy stumble
stepping out of her panties. Wolf-whistles.
She snaps, "Can't have it both ways, Dad."
And runs for the water's
cool removal. Swims out until
she turns the three of them, their matching camp hats
into a painting by Monet. Or Renoir. No sticky morning communion,
no doorway declarations, sweet clichés
can compete with this:
the care

with which he will arrange their heads
heat-heavy, on the backseat,
driving home.
Or lift the younger one
up in the air
so she can pee,
free of scratches, dirt,
scary bugs. No other mother
—hurt, hungry, wondering—
can invent opportunity
to be there
for a smaller pair of feet
to leap up from.

Pangaea

—"an ancient land mass that is thought to have split up at the end of the Palaeozoic era into the continents of Gondwanaland and Laurasia" (C20: from Greek, literally: all-earth), Collins English Dictionary

This is where we began, land
of no corners. The family united,
mountain chains undivided,
all earth mocking North or South.
One sea, one word
for land, for country,
for family.

This is where we begin, again
to melt edges
in night's rejoining:
my Northern thigh
mountained over your Southern pelvis,
burnt savannah meeting snow.
And differences of origin
collapse like your breathing,
a buzz against my neck
which sways tiny grasslands.
Nights, this is where we walk
under strange embroideries
in dreams of nakedness, one skin;
polar bears and white tigers
meeting
on the endless plains.

This is where we begin again
when morning pries us apart;
shifting continents claim their hemispheres
wrapping themselves
in icy waves, warning shores,
invisible rocks.

I wrap myself in morning kimono,
you put on your coffee,

puzzling foreheads over breakfast radio news,
we debate Quebec's separation

and startle the animals
into flight, back
to their new corners

This is where we begin:
the grounds for unity
slipping out of sight.

Photo Opportunity

They met on top of a mountain:

the proof is on her bulletin board,
edges rising like wings
in winter's dryness:

sweaty sunburn shining up her face,
the woman hiker smiles slantly, shyly
(a horsey smile, not her best side)
at this stranger catching her light
who drew her to him
by placing her within the Nikkon circle;
the bait, herself, magnified
a hundred times.

The day was a cloudless end
of October. Trick or Treat? Knees
sore, feet falling, hearts
(apparently) rising, they fumbled down
the rocky path together,
steering clear of jobs,
wives or kids, avoiding paths
they separately took
to get here. He bounced just ahead, like a boulder
checking out the best angles,
holding out her expanded image,
luring her
to heroically casual poses
at the end of a name
and phone number, quickly
pocketed in the
parking lot.

(Hiker's prophecy: the way down
is always more dangerous

than the climb up.)

Now she looks close,
deep, inside that smile. Emotional exhibitionist
turned voyeur. Warms herself
in the fading heat
of her embarrassed girl's delight. Presses up closer still, until
her image disintegrates.
And looks over her shoulder
for the magician
who turned
her laughing camera self
into a million open mouths.

The Sound of You, Forgetting Me

One hand,
folding in on its own
small chill.

In the apartmented evening,
mind restless as a cat:
something hums
above the refrigerator,
making ice.
Undiagnosed whine or ache
like a fly caught between glass:

can't let it in or out.

Next spring, it will be a tiny period
blown out
with the dusty sentence of winter.

Five thousand kilometres away
the silence is filling up
with white noise, dark worries, other
days rushing to meet you. Carefully I
have filed away
    the cards, letters, photos
you took of me
with the old year's regrets

    clear the desk, clean out
    the drawers

Still, I find
a quietness haunting
my breathing,

the sound of leaves unfolding,

one by one
before ice
       succumbs
            to river's dance.

VAUDEVILLIANS
OF TIME

Cousin Allie's Garden

I was too young
to go to her funeral,
ran across Grandfather's lawn instead, while my mother
heard how Allie dwindled her last days
in the Home, among familiar strangers:

no longer able to keep up
with her garden.
A garden where polite visitors
were lost for words,
breathless at the faith
that let a forest of leaves, branches, vines
enclose a tiny patch of lawn,
(London, Ont.),
weave all
into mystery.

Grey-green Allie, seventyish elf,
her name making me, age eight, remember

cat's eye marbles we used to covet
stashed in Crown Royal bags, lush purple–
Allie, green cat's eye
rolled quietly beneath her aisles
of tangled splendour
where ownerless cats were safe
birds harboured
invisible squirrels sprang, branches
quivering–

From backdoor to fence
it flourished,
forgiving the gardeners
who, fearful of falling
into nameless chaos,
pulled out weeds,
trimmed hedges,
imposed borders.

Here, nothing fell
but was caught
within the fabric
of Allie's embroidery:
a dropped-stitch design.

"childish," they said, "senile."
She never accepted
that someday she would have
to leave it.

But so much growth
leaping at their backfences,
finally threatened the neighbourhood:
it remembered too much.

Allie was taken away, ordered
with a neat room, bed and table,
water glass, one petunia–

and a mower was let loose
behind her back, behind her fences.

Alzheimer's is a killer, Mom sighed.

Charlie and Elsie

Maternal grandmother, Elsie Hill
(Irish maid, newly planted
in Rockglen, Saskatchewan, 1927)
living under my great-granny's roof
got appendicitis, blew up
like a bloated cow
and asked young master Charlie,
"Did you *do* something
the other night?"

He didn't accept her accusation, didn't
even believe in kissing–"swapping spits
and catching colds," he called it–
but, as a fresh CCF-er, felt sorry
for the Irish working girl,
islanded on the burnt-yellow prairie,
and married her. A step up for Elsie, he thought it,
and grand gesture, promising more,
for an idealist farmer. Except that the Depression,
which drew up cod and catfish together in its net,
rudely removed them from hope, leaving their plans
high and dry, without spawn
except for my mother and aunt, solemn-faced daughters.
Soon after Betty came, they sold up;
moved to Windsor, Ontario. Traded horse and buggy
for Ford and GM.

But Elsie never forgot that earlier island,
kept escaping back
to its social servitude. An annoyed,
genteel-poor family
always sent her "home. To your husband."

Married life became a contest. Anniversaries
should be marked with black arm bands, Elsie declared.

Once she threw potatoes (uncooked)
at her silent husband,
in raw Irish anger.
And left Charlie three times,
the last just before illness
drove her back to his door, age 64. Cancer
devoured her bowels, seat of the passions. Still
she passed on to one grandchild
her love of poetry, passion
which served her for wind-break
through life's Canadian weathers.

Charlie lived to be ninety-eight, devoted New Democrat
and still spry on his bike in the eighties,
until a wobbly left turn
into the swing of a bus, denied him the dignity
of meeting fate on his feet, like a boxer.
Instead, his last years found their focus
resisting over-worked nurses' cajoling,
tuning out his roommate's
day-long prayers to Doris,
another lost wife.

With visitors, Charlie good-naturedly guessed
at names and ages, strained to recount the story
of an ill-timed horse trade
from the most hopeful days of his life,
his young manhood and marriage.

He never mentioned
the woman who shared those years, learning
a bitter foreign soil
and beside whom he would eventually be planted,
filling a space waiting over thirty years
for that last homesteader–
belatedly, belying sentiment
but keeping up his end
of the bargain.

Baba's Donut Shop Lament

Ahh, life–whatchee gottee do?

Sitting here, almost 91 (don't tell nosy neighbours), with my oldest granddaughter–*still* unmarried. Just as well–how could *she* ever keep house, with all the books she's got to read, and write? Extravagant, careless; always leaving money on these unswept tables. Nobody ever gave me a piece of bread. Women's Liberation? I paid my way, and more. First husband gambled away the money from my land, second one spent a year in hospital after falling out of a tree I told him to prune. Third one, a heart attack. Collapsed in his boat while out fishing. Too weak, at 88, to stay with me. Men, they always leave. That's why I tell her: look out for you-self, honey.

This summer, my eyes–lidded with shadow. Big nasty crows. Cataracts operation. September, she says. If I live that long. The heat, this summer, murders me, I tell her. She swallows another piece of donut, nodding. Taps her fingers, bored. Thank God for *Mr. Donut*, I say–even if the donuts *are* stale. The clerk, a nice Chinaman, is polite and waits, when I stand at the counter, clutching my heart from the furnace outside.

She says: *Well, why don't you let us get you an air conditioner, then? Lots of people in your building have those window-units. Then you could monitor the temperature in your apartment. Climate control. Wouldn't you like that?* Throws a bunch of words at me, sinks back. I have to take a breath, a sip of coffee, and tell her: *Don't be giving your Father foolish ideas, my dear. I don't want to worry for that–I already have to watch out for television, stove, fridge. So, no. No. No more machines.*

She bangs her cup down, folds her arms on the table, and looks at me, waiting. Sulky. After all I've done...what's the reward, God? Even this lump they call a donut has no taste, the vegetables are like plastic, and I can't find anything in this noisy, smelly city to fit me– everything's shrinking. Except the bunions. Won't be able to wear the white shoes we found today, until October. If I live that long.

She always asks how I'm doing, and what can I say? The truth: everyday, everyday, I go down. Now she fidgets and gazes at the people passing on the sidewalk outside. Tugs at an earring; looks like a spider crawling up her neck. Hair wild like a teenager's this summer. Too skinny, too. I ask her, When are you gonna be like a *normal* lady? She growls, stares over my head. When did they stop looking at me? I sigh *Ah well...maybe I die tomorrow. Then you won't have to put up with Baba, no more.* She pats my arm, says, *After all you've suffered...you've been so strong, you've got to believe....* and stops, lifting her small white hands. Empty hands.

My granddaughter's a scholar, and she has lots of books stored away in her head. But I know it wasn't worth it: never worth it, my heart.

The Generations: Visiting his Family

First night, going to bed
in his parents' damp basement, semi-
finished, long-term project,
we sank into a lumpy pull-out, stain-patterned,
soggy as steamed toast. Inhaling
his buttery heat, I pulled
his boy's body over me
like a robe. Yet lay hungrily awake after,
haunted by household darkness,
teased by the oddly
familiar air.

Next day, sniffing out his early terrain,
we traced the easy pattern
of the street's quiet crescent
curving back upon itself
as we were returned to where we began:
three-bedroom bungalow, tiny sprinklered yard,
fresh-painted porch before
the "company-only"
front door
where we sat, and argued marriage.

Here he is reborn, reclaimed
as son, brother, grandson. Their touching
re-making of him (childhood ailments, toys and pranks)
presented to me as a home-made gift.
Home-made cookies are also in the jar for me,
reminder of the childish sweet tooth
I can't lose.

His father, father-like, casually herds us
towards meal time and daily routine,
amusing headlines read out
in my direction. He has his son's lankiness,

made weedy with age.
Puffball of hair
keeps him a kidder.
His mother, perfect. As if
she came with the house,
perfect, modest, neat. Tiny whiskers
at the corners of her mouth
frame her gentle smile with a hint
of feline. Intelligence also glints
behind her skill at listening;
Manitoba farmer's toughness, softened
by aproned hips and belly,
testimonies of domestic content.

I sit with her in the kitchen,
woman with woman
(but crunching on her cookies),
while her son, thirty-one,
down in the basement, exercises
an injured knee: narrative of worry, she is aware,
now borne by his newest woman.

Meanwhile her husband rides his three-speed
on his daily jaunt
around the neighbourhood's cottonwoods and kids,
circling them again in his report, afterwards,
to whoever is in the kitchen, waiting, listening.

Meatloaf and mashed completes the journey
on which we, hopeful clumsy family,
meet the potholes and petunias
of another twenty-four, tying
dawn to dusk; journey
as familiar, forgiving and resisted
as the musty embrace of the pull-out
after dark: drawing us down
into the clinging arms
of the generations.

Power Interruption

12:00 12:00 12:00

flashing doomsday digits,
microwave and VCR tell us

time

has been erased.

Mom bangs down her cup. "Damnit!
Third time this week."

Late August, the escape I craved–
hum of air conditioner suspended,
afternoon holds its breath
on the verge of a sigh
that will shiver the poplar leaves,
blow sunlit dust
from desks and teachers and tests. Waiting
to sharpen my mind
with my marking pencils,
I have come to this house
for childhood's cup of comfort
and find our white-tiled kitchen
become a hot, grease-spotted cave,
wrapped in shadow. Edging towards
itch-scratching of argument,
we are struggling ants
fixed in amber, staring
at frozen hands
of the kitchen clock
Mom used to set ahead ten minutes
to hasten morning take-off
before we caught on, lengthened the runway.

Who has the power
to stop time? Well, the mysterious men
who dug up the sidewalk front
have interrupted the serpent Midgard's coiled sleep
and we are caught, moths
opening ourselves on pins,
in stale afternoon light,
somewhere between the relentless rowing
of the second hand and digital shift,
those homely markers that drive our lives
behind necessary fences. Like our ten thousand
walks, thirty years worth,
which have surely shifted
concrete blocks of sidewalk by now,
along with the continents. The return
to our storm door, each time
a prayer
to the welcome smallness of our lives.

Are we small enough, even
to escape the eye of the clock?
Slipping between
the cracks
like ants
that have invaded our kitchen?
Dad, our Schweitzer
flying them out
on newspaper planes or the lip
of a glass tumbler. Mom,
shocked every time, cruelly brings down
her fading pink slippers.

Quickly, quickly restore
the grim figures
clicking their way through space
that assure us life
will go on, the same way, hour by hour
as we chase our footsteps. That our stumbled paths

will reach out and guide us
even as we fall,
out of time.

So I sit with them in the dark, sticky kitchen
and wait for the power
to come back on. Civic certainty
seesawing with cave-dweller's fear.
Noticing the veins
winding across my mother's hands
as she lifts her cold cup;
the smallness my father
has recently embraced, at sixty-nine
as he gets up and lifts the blind
to watch starlings swoop and swerve
around the plastic Zeller's birdbath.

We wait.

Black wings pass across the window,
fickle August light
drawing us in and out of shadow.

two photos of god

one: His

out-of-focus, fish eye's view:

bulging from the corner,
my father's stern face
swims to surface.
Careful combings of hair, one
partially-blind eye
staring up, glasses removed
for the camera. Sharp
nose, well-scraped cheek,
and tightened lips
forecast judgment. Behind him
an uncurtained window, holding hint
of flash's lightning,
before the pall of
night, descending.

two: Hers

an unexpected angel of vision—

photographer jumped, two feet
too high

capturing instead
half her regal head
blue October sky,
puffy with cumulus, curling above
dark beauty-parlour swirls
of my mother's still-natural brown,
cut off at the bangs. Uncrowned queen,
she is hiding beneath the frame,
saving her happiness
for unseen generations:

light, ascending.

the toothbrush

My battered knapsack a stowaway
to L.A.   or Tokyo,
courtesy of Air Canada, I arrive home, ten at night
without even that: imagine

the nakedness. Milky tea and cookies
seal and sweeten the return
in their clock-ticking kitchen,
where I take a burning gulp,
awkwardly   spit out
my request

and the old instinct
to nurture and protect
even overgrown offspring
brings an embarrassment of riches:

my father finds one or two,
"barely used," at the bottom
of his dresser drawer;
my mother puzzles the pedigree
of several brushes
not yet consigned
to spring cleaning

each one marked by the mouth
of its owner, bristles bending
to mulishness of flesh and enamel,
the blinkered plod of daily hygiene.

(Dental records
offer us ghostly fingerprints
after the body has disappeared. Shoes
haunt the hallway. Toothbrush
waits beside the sink; tube, half-used,

keeping your grip.)

Finally, choosing one at random
and purifying it with peppermint,
I take it into my mouth

reviving memories
of the days of skinless infancy

sharing heat, milk, blood

Like any other nestling, I willingly
swallow
their undigested love.

photographing the Moose: 3 snapshots
snapshot #1

If a moose shits in the woods,
does anybody see?

We witnessed its tribute to earth
one weekend, both halves of a 14 K hike
as our gazes caressed forest floor
seeking roots, ankle-seducing boulders, rodent holes,
sighting those neat nests of carmel buttons
casually deposited
every few meters
so that we looked around corners of rise and rock
for the long-legged pollutants
whose excrement became our trophy,
our hiking-boot souvenirs:
but only the moose dung cooperated
for our camera,
piled beside God's dirty laundry
of April snow.

snapshot #2

A pile-up of cars, misty July afternoon
signals not a spill of bodies across the twisting Cabot highway
missing lives and tomorrow's headlines
but a crowd of photographers, families, campers
getting their fix–and we all stumble out
of vans and RVs,
air-conditioned bubbles of boredom
weary of repeating cliffs and waves
like an NFB travelogue on Pause,
to stare at the well-carpeted backside
of marsh-browsing moose.
Indifferent to our calls, waves and shutter-clicking,
moving just enough to prove no mirage.

After two hours in the coastal near-rain,
backseat bargaining and back-home dreaming,
we find communal focus
in this blurring, unconcerned image
which eats on,
at the center of our hunger.
Cameras raised in unison,
we put a box between ourselves
and the god; filter the wilderness
with a tiny glass eye.
And stand beside
neighbouring strangers
whose licenses, accents, languages
sealed us, earlier, within tribal skin
to laugh, grin, greet and point
as the unaffected hillock of brown fur, velveted rack
consumes summer, head barely lifting
to acknowledge his acolytes.

Gravel crunches. One last car
rolls up–a park car, by the logo–and the woman
who cleans the bathrooms
we meet at every night,
to brush teeth, use toilets, compare days,
leans out, nods at the crowd, saying,
"Oh that's just Harold. He comes here everyday."

snapshot #3

An easy death,
that's what my husband calls it,
as we stare at the trailer
Highway 11, south from Temagami:
the flapping red tarp half-reveals
carcass of a moose, its hooves now pawing sky,
tied down beside the ATV.
Swamp donkey. I want to close my eyes, first,

if not those. Cloven feet stir in the wind, restlessly.
Wolves, or starvation, he says,
sooner or later. Not many moose
die of old age. I start to argue; swallow.
Rack of antlers on the rec room wall: *still life*. I sigh. Swallow.
Suddenly truck, trailer and moose pull out, between
transports, drop us behind with a roar—
just as I was thinking of my camera.

Vaudevillians of Time

"The sixth age shifts
Into the lean and slipper'd pantaloon...."
–Shakespeare, *As You Like It*

All right: it's been said–
something about the seven ages of humanity
and the riddle of the Sphinx–
better in blank verse, Sophocles' chorus,
than bitten-off chuckles
of family jokes-cum-anecdotes,
delivered with axiomatic laughter.

But there's the moment when his father,
recovered, much smaller,
from five weeks denied his wife's baking,
pricked and prodded in hospital,
stopped after *Horton's*
to unlock the mailbox
and his pants   fell down.
Fumbled to drag up his respectability
–just after the neighbour's friendly honk, and wave–
hide the yellowing shorts
the Missus nagged him to throw out,
while standing at the door, she yodelled
"'Y' remember the milk, Hon?"

Or the moment when his mother
a month after knee surgery,
put on her husband's old Sorels
and staggered through February snow to retrieve
a wind-blown blue-box. Dragging it,
slipped, fell down:
turtled in the foot-deep snow,
her new metal knees locked
so that she cursed and sputtered

and morning commuters whizzed by
a foot from her self-dug hollow
until the neighbour's dog sniffed over
let her drag herself up
on his dirty yellow fur, soaked and growling.

And her mother
who volunteered to take the six-year-old
through the Carnival Funhouse, declaiming
before the bored lineup:
"She shouldn't have to go by HERSELF!"
Once shut up in the dark corridor
the floor split into panels, lifting, then dropping,
mocking her steps, causing breath
to stick in her mouth, and legs
to separate: one above, one below, clinging to the life-raft
she could neither get on nor climb off–
granddaughter skipping ahead, while half-falling, she calls to no one
"Turn it off, please–I'm stuck!"
A shadow appears beside her
seizes a lever, bangs it down, so all is still
except for the disappointed wail of children,
and he drags her out, like a citizen's arrest,
never letting go her trembling wrist.
"Can we do it again, Grandma?" someone shouts
far below
as the world spins around her, grinning.

Or even: *me*
beginning the historic fire tower climb
all four of us,
bringing the three-year-old along
with a firm grip on her hand, saying
"One step at a time–don't rush–Mom's got you"
And at the third landing
where it begins to climb
in an inverted gyre
wind lifts the girl's summer dress

hats are threatened
and more and more of the forest below peeks through,
glimmer of lakes, shining, vertigo
and the child says,
"Just a little further Mom,"
pulling her up–
and there is only trust
as they reach the top
and Mom wipes her neck,
crouching under the lookout
while the kids jump up to see
the parking lot, their green van,
beckoning like a lake.

What is this seltzer in the face,
finger in the eye,
the clown's endless slide toward ignominy
on a giant banana peel
done without laugh track or applause?
The Sphinx has been answered
Oedipus is blind
and given enough time,
we are the punch-line.

ICEBERG
RIDER

Iceberg Rider

Though cold rises into his bones,
he will steer it: sold, twenty-five-year-
old house, lurching south
to its final dissolve
in pacific shallows
of a late-life divorce.
Family dream—nuclear—
and illusion of unity,
drifting
to the final meltdown.

All winter he patrolled
these empty bedrooms. Protecting our
neglected treasure, trashed
in drawers, closets and basement.
Caretaker
of a long-haunted house, watching while
ghosts become noisier, living
paler, fading off into excuses,

labels, accusations. *"Dysfunctional Family."*
"Delayed Mid-Life Crisis. "
"Fin-de-Siecle Angst."
Pushing through Atlantic
ice storms of ending,
meetings with lawyers
and real estate agents—
carrion crows
circling, measuring
his dwindling island.
Navigating, day by day,
the narrowing path
from dark bedroom to bathroom, kitchen
and back—caves he pierces
with storm lanterns
of peasant fatalism. If you don't
give yourself any extra
ground, he tells me, home for the last mile,
you're grateful enough
to keep walking. But at night,
I know, listening,
how he struggles for his footing,
feels the bulk of a quarter century
rocking below. Groaning, declaring its weight,
invisible
under green sealight of sailor's day
aboard the ship
of melting ice.

Visiting, I note how he's kept all
clean as a hotel, surfaces shiny
and slick.
Clutter she hated, gone:
clearing the decks, he calls it.
(Only our ghosts, at eight, at fifteen,
at twenty, getting louder
the heavier the quiet, closing in
as we stand, silent

at the window. Screaming
like gulls, chasing the ice.)

At last, with bays and sounds
        opening   all around us,
ice settling deeper in southering waves,
gulls swooping, crying
Out There,
Out There–
we go down with the ship.
Sink beneath
the waving horizon. Our core
consumed by
austral walls
of bitter salt.

"Life is Maintenance"

my father said, day after I moved back
into my girlhood bedroom, summer of '95.
Crying for my childhood, I tried to burrow
deep into its cave
of rain-scented summer days,
before books were written
by people I taught, but merely mysteries
carved on my heart.
Tried to write papers, read criticism, and
stop assigning grades to every philosophy that walked by.

Mormon "elders" of twenty-two, smiling at the door
twice in one month, I gave a 'C+' for earnest effort,
Dad $2.00. Only my mother
gave them a hearing, their touching ties and crew-cuts,
filling our book-scattered living room
with stories of apocalypse
("So handsome!").

Air conditioner gave out
after five days of 30-degree heat, dishwasher
sprang a leak, rubber bumpily unravelled
on the tires of our Volvo,
and my parents' thirty-six-year-old marriage
came undone.

          * * *

Flipping through the box of unsellable records, between
embarrassment and antique–
Ziggy Stardust, Captain Fantastic,
The Grand Illusion, Bridge over Troubled Water,
Teaser and the Fire Cat–
ten years of dark moons, oily circles
which spun adolescents

into late-night necking sessions,
then morning-after languor
bathing in replayed lust,
prostrated on the couch. Laundry basket full, waiting
at my feet. Romance
is high school's invention,
all elbows, acne, agony. Each fingering of nostalgia
("the hits of yesterday and today")
unlocks a tiny door to eighteen, fifteen–
no matter the disco drone
(Donna Summer, Bee Gees,
plastic posturing of Queen or Styx)
when I put stylus to tortured vinyl
and lie back on the squeaky couch,
I tunnel into those never-ending
make-out sessions, the testing of new
boundaries, sweetness of blank bodies
we were so anxious to rewrite.

Now inked with initials not our own, of heartache
and age: Sit up, rub knee ache, Aerobics memento. Mom
has joined a Seniors exercise class in her building, Dad announces,
letting go of the phone
 while the record skips, keeps
on keeps on skipping–

     * * *

This year, I paid a lawyer
to draw up my will. "Now, the door is open,"
Dad approves, then shows
his copy of the Separation Agreement,
and I nod, not adding that the door reads, "EXIT."
Maggots are just the larval stage of houseflies,
moving from one habitation to another,
after all. And my old boyfriend/bestfriend
and lately, "personal consultant,"
drives off to the West Coast

in a loaded-down Japanese import–
the year after I returned
in a second-hand station wagon
belonging to my maintenance-man lover:
I paid, both ways.

* * *

Today, through the patio door glass,
I watch my father fill up the plastic birdbath
Mom bought at Zeller's, two months before
she decided to take her own apartment.
(Their thirty-sixth anniversary, a month ago:
unmarked blank on the calendar.) Welcoming robins,
jays, cardinals, waxwings
who splash, grateful, day after sun-devilled day.
"You've got to take care of something,"
he says, toting the watering can back
to the laundry room
where his shirts wait,
stretched across
the ironing board.
He fingers cuffs, collars,
lamenting–the ring
never comes out
despite years of her scrubbing.

Separating: 36 Years

I Loam Sweet Loam

Now that my mother's moved out,
a tiny apartment in a Co-op building,
suggested by her women's group
("a bunch of nagging Noras
who've worn out their own marriages, and want company"),
my father is cleaning out the fridge
tossing away hoarded scraps, servings and spoonfuls
that she reshaped into Sunday evening "tea,"
which we thudded downstairs for, always late, complaining and amazed:
rigid jello for her diet, half-sour prunes for his digestion,
styrofoam take-out dishes of fried rice and potato salad,
one unclaimed fortune cookie, stale buns saved
for bread crumbs to stuff into a ceremonial bird.
"All I can think is,
what did I do to deserve this: a wife
who leaves me after thirty-six years."
(Me, re-sweeping the floor, eyes
on invisible dust.) Slamming out the side door,
he takes it all
to the composter, plastic accepting maw
he's been faithful to, without issue, on our lot's gravel-sand,
for twenty summers. Then covers our kitchen sins
with soft black loam, meeting threats of
rabid raccoons, rain, new owners' curiosity,
all potential grave robbers.
"Loam sweet loam," he says,
tossing blackness down
over another ending, of left-over
beginnings, briefly interrupting
dance of worms, house flies, maggots
of our ravenous imagination.

―――――

II   Coming Clean

Today I helped him
put up shower curtains
he had washed. The once-a-year job
Mom did without mentioning,
surprising us with fresh light,
vinyl veiled, falling gently
upon our nakedness. Sails that rose
and fell around us, riding out
monsoonal rain, polar spray,
sweat and oil that lined the tiles,
rough weather of our bodies, journeying
blindly, towards deeper waters.

This summer, Dad is fighting back,
furiously scouring surfaces
cleaning closets and emptying drawers.
"Hate messes. One cup,
one plate, a few utensils, that's all I need.
Why wash so many dishes? Why clean
so many towels?"

Standing together in the Master bathroom,
which I only use, still, with a furtive feeling
of trespass, flesh's family knowledge
registered by tub ring and toilet water mark,
he said
I dreamt I was caught
in the cross-fire. You know,
a shoot-out. Fighting for my life. Handing up the curtain rings
to my perch on tub edge,
he is shirtless for the August heat, skin-tide
lapping around his neck,
shoulders speckled like a barnacled hull,
scrapbooked from days thrilled as
sun-daring pale sailor, Russian-born

who walked above Lake Michigan, and knew only
that humans sink, so stay out
of the water.
He hands me the last ring.
I'd rather not sleep than dream
like that. Wake up feeling so sweaty, so dirty.
With rage. Voice sinks, *like filth, you know. Like—shit.*
I step down, nodding. Swallowing
bitter aftertaste, like from your first
adult drink, coffee or beer. I own an extra inch,
as he stands now, pants slipping down
over square feet that didn't know shoes
until Canada, age eight. *Great—and I'm just ready*
for that shower, you know. He pats my shoulder
as I slip out, the door closed
between us again, sea wall
that used to be enough,
and an ocean-going wind howls in my ear:
how much smaller
and cleaner
we will both be
when his sails finally
get taken in, and the curtain
comes down.

on the treadmill

6 a.m.
A crow rasps ownership over the suburb,
towering pines that top the house,
soon to be handed over to the new occupants,
with plans of pruning, and jacuzzis.

My father coughs, and on the other side of the house,
I roll out of dreaming. June is for brides. Today is their ghost
anniversary–the thirty-seventh they never saw, together.
So he vows to add thirty-seven
to his seventy, despite the cough, and the dizziness
that stops him in his tracks on regular walks
round the neighbourhood he watched grow
from rows of matchstick trees and raw yards
with blond children sitting in kiddie pools.
Now quick foreign chatter, warm colours, strange
gatherings of whispering fabric, passing him on the sidewalk,
spice its Wonder Bread blandness. His aching lungs,
tight chest, preserving, as he gasps, the faint
scent of saffron.

He rises, dresses in yesterday's shirt–sweat glands
have dried up this year–and goes downstairs
for the glass of orange juice he left out last night
so the burst of citrus won't freeze his fillings.
Little shocks must be avoided now.

Ghosts track him through the house–of children,
shrieking assaults on the furniture and one another.
Of teenagers, sprawling on the floor, whispering
laughter, *Oh my Gods,* phone nested
in their unwashed hair. Of lovers, on the couch
winding around each other and waves of Queen,
Styx, Elton John. "Someone saved my life tonight."

This afternoon, the second stress test.
A girl with green fingernails has him step
onto a treadmill. After five leaden minutes, stops him:
he stares, cotton-lunged: success or failure? Breath
returning, verdict deferred. The doctor
will call him next week, she says, making
a mark on his chart. He drives home, legs trembling
at every red. Late that night, as he wrestles
with sleep, he still feels the pull he must resist,
gravity, the force of the machine tugging
against watery muscles. Floor rolling,
running, jumping. Stealing his strength, maleness,
his youth. Lungs aching, sweat seeping. Edge creeping ever
closer, teasing his heels with dark oceans,
as he cries out his wife's name, from some
lost day of islands, soft hands. Clutches instead
the corner of the bed and
another long day is launched
in the hoarse dark mocking
sheltered by the trees he had planted.

grounding

I want to say,
A woman needs a basement,
but the language won't let me
claim the liberation
of this honest dark lowering:

the fact is, downstairs, below,
holding up my house
is a space permeated by worms, plants, spring storms
mice and mould and silverfish
a forced understanding
I must stoop to enter,
our kinship with dirt, the damp, the spider
and the rust. Roots, do I have roots—
one is poking thorough the damp rubble wall,
eyeless albino beggar infiltrating
fifty-year-old foundations, this home we've not built
but accepted, accommodated, entered into knowing,
correcting and defending
like a problem child. Our continual beginning,
our faith in it, ourselves, and all that it sustains
is seen in the past visions we bury here—
ski boots, camping pots, tent pegs, lifejackets,
Christmas lights, a stereo eternally holding *Ella and Louis*
unplaying the twentieth century,
 boxes and bags ready for future frugality,
old skates and saw blades and styrofoam packing
fraying badminton rackets, damp baseball gloves,
games that we may return to
some mythic summer, piles of possessions
we're not quite ready to surrender
to the crass neighbourhood battling for failures and secrets
of Saturday morning yard sales,
or abandon to landfill and the groaning pits
tumoured with our earthly mistakes,

our helpless taking-up-of-space—

This spring day, I give myself the pleasure
of uncovering basement, discovering
damp cracking cement, uprising earth, corner rivers,
where the winter mice play and leave
commas of disdain for our dreams of containment.

My father held his frenzied yearly purge here,
 carnival of cleaning,
this space no one personally owned or cared for, except him:
space for both drying laundry and hidden liquor bottles,
"old country" suitcases, rejected wedding presents
and the toys we never played with. Our childhood basement:
used one year for painting lessons,
another for hockey, or boxing, ritualizing our rages,
a weight bench to lie back on, press angry arms
towards kitchen floorboards, where our mother muttered
over the soggy dishtowel.
Then the museum of our student years,
the books, the futons, the framed posters, beanbags in black leather;
then remnants of Baba's reign, the fifty-year old tables,
three-quarter beds, boxes of hand-embroidered pillow cloths,
dresser slips for our non-existent hope chests. And floating on top,
our family home's last summer, empty boxes—waves
of red-lettered ALLIED VAN LINE vessels, free
of charge, thrown in with the moving contract, post-divorce.

Each spring, he'd pile and pile,
shout up the stairs, his movements getting brisker,
more efficient each hour, each trip
for water, bags and sponge mops,
and finally, by suppertime, call us to come and see
what ghosts he had laid to rest, to proudly display
funeral pyres of our past selves, dreamed selves
disowned, drifting or drowned selves.
The garbage truck next day

stuffed all into its hydraulic maw
while the new naked floor would be flooded:
for a morning of mopping, barefoot Cinderellas,
we swept the swamp
back down the dark mouths of drains, to the worms, beetles, dirt—
woke the next day to the blank infant face
of a shiny new start,
the returning rainbow covenant.
"Now let's keep it this way," he'd say, each time—
though smudges of uncovered feet,
darkened his victory.
And as I sort
and sweep and bury and pile and exclaim, adrenaline-surging,
tripping over bags and piles half-completed
to start another,
pushing back the tide once more
I carry his legacy:
we spring-mad basement-cleaners
are holding our ground.

Night Light

Household beacon, your bed-side lamp
fixes the whole of the bedroom
in an evening glow. Touches
your forest of paperbacks,
stacks of magazines, neatly read;
outlines the double-knot twisting
in the counterpane
on the bed, becalmed
at centre. (Glossy new companion
rests on the empty side.)
Welcoming craft
at the ends of your days, it's lapped
by soft, aging shadows, sheets drawn
for your arrival, library sailor.

The imminence of arrival
signalled by the light,
everything in the room
—your newest bottle of Old Spice, packets of violin strings,
cloth handkerchiefs, dusty photos on the dresser
(your father grinning outside his shack,
graduation pictures of my sister, me;
a heavy-eyed young man who was yourself),
old watches waiting
new time to keep—
is washed in amber,
pulled into waves of night
heading for the empty bed.

Here, your presence, promised
to the future, to night,
becomes a promise to me, bookish daughter

pausing on the dark landing,
a pledge of future presents,
a light waiting,
and, after so many night passages,
pages yet to be turned.

WHEN HER THIGHS WERE PERFECT

When Her Thighs Were Perfect

Well, once
they were measured
in hot quick glances
from sun-gilded cars
booming hormonal thunder.
Artemis, the huntress:
she could walk on those legs
right out of herself,
dizzy with breath,
opening the new page
on agonizing drives home,
in sticky lingering embrace
of a cranked-down bucket-seat;
marathon petting sessions
in her parents' driveway,
or the parking lot
of a "Kiss and Ride."
Tiny gold leg-hairs
tingling, pre-razor,

flesh finger-smudged.
Still carries
the shadow of bliss
that seared her,
first bristly male kisses,
hands climbing knees—
before she slammed
the passenger door,
almost four. Smoothed
down her shorts,
erasing. Then the hall
light came on, and her father
put his slippered foot
on the stair.

Fifteen years later, she learns to read
a new chapter of travel and time,
mapping her flesh with "You Are Here."
Future destinations
pointed out by her sisters, moving on with
or without drivers. Asphalt waiting,
and the father's vigil, over;
the whole road is now hers.

Yet when blushes are only applied with brushes
and she thickened against the ritual quills
of husbands out for the evening, howling
with the pack that turns
at the goddess's whim, she aches
for an untouched page
to turn over, embracing
its muteness. Settles instead
for the lab report, brought
like a bouquet of roses by knowing lovers

declaring all negative.

The Bikini Stomach

one hundred sit-ups a day
ought to do it—

so she, at seventeen,
and 118 (lbs.)
her body splintered
into strips and segments of restless continents,
tectonic plates shifting under
new figure-fault lines,
never quite ready for
the red bikini her mother bought her.

-the legs, okay. Started shaving last summer,
revealing smooth-beached islands of calf, thigh
-the breasts, thank God, were there
at last (fifteen—ancient!)
-the ass, she couldn't really be sure
if it was too big or too small,
three way mirrors never told,
flashing salesgirl sarcasm,
so buying jeans
was a seasonal agony,
but it wasn't in front of her, anyway—

but when she discovered this softly curving
other protrusion, cushioning, rounding
out her profile, storing the day's surplus,
she became obsessed with its discipline
("pot belly," "baby fat")
as magazines promised "The Bikini Stomach,"
covers featuring ectomorphic teens, glossed by *Glamour*
proudly emptied of flesh and pimple-innocent.
Eradicate this ultimate indignity,
the belly, pouch of lazy flesh
internal seepage carried under clothes

like a tumour or wound. Watched
people on buses, the street,
amazed, ashamed that they, too,
bore this shadow of weakness.
Beneath even the girdles
of her mother's day, "control-top" pantyhose
of her own. No surgical removal
of the longed-for femaleness now possible,
no reconciliation with roundness
away from mirrors and magazines,
could be allowed: true lines only,
no latitude. Late night teeth-gritted determination
when she hooked feet under the dresser,
crunching up, grunting, banishing softness
in the flannel nightgown, pink
(now reddening with sweat, new rising scent)
Baba gave her, scolding her granddaughter
as "too skeeny—wassamatter you girls, you
weak, or someting? Here, have meatball
and cabbage rolls, then pie." The memory
lifts her as she sinks back, gasping:
of giving in, sitting down
at Baba's table, feeling her map of borders collapse,
as she breathed out again. The lined hand, bringing food,
touched her hair, shining

while she stared back at herself, age two, age ten,
in photos still centred on Baba's bureau
under the ticking clock. Sky-eyed curious girl
restlessly dressed,
by her mother, leans forward
or stretches out
burning to burst through frames

and she picks up a fork, leans back,
waxing moon softly nesting in her lap:

the world again, become whole.

The Wedding Hair-Do

Who planted this ornamental shrub
on top of my head? Twenty-three hair-pins,
half a bottle of spray, and I reach up, feel
nylon wires of a flexible bird cage, towering
behind my back. Women comfortable
with the arsenal of hair spray, gel and mousse
took my head in their hands for an hour,
eased me of its weight, inside;
substituted another. Scolded me
for split ends, hair dryers on high, swimming pools,
slipping into Price-Cutters between groceries
and laundry, for "just the minimum."

I came in for "the minimum," then, softened
by wedding frenzy, my mother's contagious dreams,
(the rehearsal she hopes this is)
shyly blurted "do something
wedding-like with it...Put it up, maybe?"
Making at last, the dreamed debutante's
entrance: hair up, skirts down, like a lady.

And so my shoulder-length summer hay
is made captive to irons and rollers and dryers,
victim of a vision out of *Ladies Home Journal*
or *Cinderella* by Disney. Curled, teased, pinned
sprayed into submission.
When they silently lift the glass, capturing
the new garden of *terra incognita*, back of my head,
I can only say, "Uh, thanks—it's very—different."
Pat, and muse: poodle, or Barbara Eden's "Jeanie"?
In the plaza, the drug store, the A & P
I think everyone is staring.
"I'm going to a wedding," I gurgle
to the pregnant checkout girl. Like explaining away
a black eye, shameful result of losing some contest,

with exaggerated accounts of the strength
of the opposition. (She tells me I "look sweet.")
I come home to my parents' applause, in chorus for once.
Before I go, Dad takes my picture–their "princess"
at last *(sans* Prince; between tales). Bite down
on my laughter, remembering how beauty
contestants, before the cameras, would sink teeth
into pencilled red lips
to make them still redder.

But next morning, singing in the shower, post-Cinderella's midnight
I flatten again all hopes
under soapy ownership of
my head. Pile of hair pins
glinting by the sink:
nobody's slipper to fill, only the shiny signs
    of the bird's latest escape.

Easter in North Bay

I   Good Friday

all the wounded bodies
of the women
descend into water:

(Aquabics Class)

proud to be still sleek in my Speedo
and in the front row of exercisers, I
jump and splash and churn
my own yearnings toward perfection
into blue-white spray
fogging the high windows
looking out on the Station,
winter's sullen retreat.

Betty's had a mastectomy, Suzanne
a CAT scan. Marie's wearing a new bathing suit
and talks of planting annuals. Time's writing,
that begins by punctuating blank girl's skin
on buttocks and thighs,
has autographed their bodies
with cursive of scar tissue. Stretch
marks. Age spots. Ink-blots of veins.
Visitations of weakness, pain.
Yet the women welcome
each other with laughter,
making room for the ripple
of another body, lifting the level
as class begins. Joining
the circle, later, to move walls of water,
we smile, gasp and laugh
against our collective force,
which could split a chlorine sea.

Like extras in an Esther Williams movie,
we kick together furiously now,
shouting, counting off,
until the ceiling tiles silver.
Fingers at our throats
panting, as we finish,
marking the strength
of our ineluctable blood.
And thank the instructor, after
with footnotes on
children's planned marriages,
husband's slow recoveries,
sure signs of spring–
while bosomy floral-suit
leads bird-hipped stroke victim,
down the steps, past me
each bathed inch awakening
as I climb back to earth:

in the steam of the showers,
my sisters,
I'll follow you

|| Easter Sunday

Walking to the Laundromat
I carry my sins in a white bag,
Santa-style, over my shoulder.

(with one exception:

the sins of the non-mothers
are visited on the daughters
who dip stained cotton,
despite best intentions of kotex,

into punishing cold water
alone, at home
chastened panties flung
over the shower rail.
Smudged cloth my mother once hid
from my brother's eyes:
"He shouldn't have to see that.")

Now, cross the corner, pass
Pro Cathedral of the Assumption,
ballasting iceberg of belief
fronting waves of atheistic traffic.
A blood donor clinic, today
will be held in the basement:
inverse communion?

Walk on. Dump before the laundress, chain-smoking Mary,
seven days of sweat and smells, shame
and soil, weakness of the body. Life's
leakage, how it spills
over borders. The humiliation of witnessing
is lessened only
by her forgiving sex.

Confessed in the margins of my days,
my sins will soon wind down
the soap-clogged drain
and in two hours I will unpack
sweet bundles of cloth,
to rise again, in the flesh.

On the way back, I stop at the Cathedral.
"Are you on our list, dear?"
Shake my head,
receive a new white card
and exchange my address for a place in line
among truckers, students, waitresses
known again as neighbours.

A thumb-prick discovers the universal donor.
Soon my right-hand vein
nurses a needle
in an urge for sainthood,
greedy for sweetness doled out
by Red Cross-habited volunteers:
cookies and Pepsi and "Dear"'s.

Arm extended, new wound whispering
among the others lying beside me.
Look up at the faces of those waiting their turn,
feet quiet on the scarred floor, talking spring.
Look up at white coats and lipstick,
red-lipped flowers
of women's saving faces, the forgiving
carriers of the race. While the blood, koolaid-coloured, seeps
into a bag hidden beneath. Life's leakage. Precious red surplus
—like spawning salmon, filling the streams
like October leaves, washed into the gutters—
joining above with below,
a crimson umbilical. We rediscover
our colour
before we abandon it. Around me, neighbours rise,
fingers on the new opening,
led gently to a table
where strangers breathe quietly, pass
the Peek Freans and grape juice.

A pat on the shoulder, a breath of
Lily of the Valley. "Are you still
with us, dear?"
And I smile, look up: "Yes."

Looking for My Inner Bitch

The dog thinks we are a pack,
not a family–
my husband the alpha male,
who can flip her on her tail, kneel
on her thick throat until she pants forth
meaty miasma and pleading tongue, legs
lashing the broadloom, sending out
feathers of black fur
while belly balloons, paws scrabble,
adoring the dominator
in silent fawning.

Since I remain quietly on the couch
with book or pen
tea and newspaper,
she bares her teeth at me,
indifferent to vet's bills paid,
dogfood stockpiled,
license clinking like a bell on her neck
When I come downstairs
mornings, to push her outside,
naked under flannel nightgown,
furless shanks and buttocks
chilled at the January door–
she growls, refuses to leave the couch
to recognize my calls, schoolteacherish repeating
of her name
for I am a squirrel, a rodent, without teeth
or claws. I flee
up the stairs, find, instead,
a hockey stick. Return
to thump the floor, and growl–
only then does she slink off, drop down
creep out on the yellow-stained snow,
reluctantly lowering female parts
onto cold crust, to release her stream.
Looking back over her shoulder
as if she knew how to wink.

PERSONAL EFFECTS

after he goes

fetishist magazines
sprawl brazenly
beside Milan Kundera   Mark Twain
Times Literary Supplement. unmated
socks, last summer's shorts,
are protecting still-opened books.
musky T-shirts hiding
inside sweaters.
these, and many other
offences against nature—

so after he goes
I do the laundry,
purify faithful towels
that swamp with our stickiness

and when I'm done, pile
his (clean) undershorts, socks,
T-shirts, books and magazines

(the very bottom)
neatly, in his corner.

now chaste pairs
of cups and plates
stacked by the sink
testify to single needs
and modest meals
eaten with book in hand
    a *crunch crunch*   a page turned
    a moment spent

but VISA slips
of last spring's owing
still drift from his desk
furtively, like April snow

Canadian Tire money he forgets
folded into my books,
warning me
of lost opportunity;
the smell of his pillow
is a river I slide into,
turning to the dark.

with a spin of this crazy wheel,
he brings the chaotic
into my life, this messy apartment
my heart

emotional vision sharpened
by distance,
I am dazzled by silent evidence
of so many rebirths,
so many shed skins
shining where they rest

sheened by our dust.

Lines

that Line he drew
between us

yesterday's hot slow afternoon
sitting in a park
filled up with lovers

is repeated by
line of sunburn, today

dividing my cotton-sheltered ankles
from naked pleading knees

the lost sock, or loneliness at the laundromat

Reaching through piles
of warm cotton and polyester
breathing in my basket,
I pair sleeves and mate socks,
my dresser Noah's ark, until I come
to the lost sheep, the lone wolf,
darkly singular, and
curled like a question mark:
what went wrong? Who upset the balance
of dualities, the partnering
of left with right?
And think of my parents, each
in 1-bedroom apartments as the year ends
with its shipwreck and flotsam. A wound
in the fabric of my childhood,
leaving a hole where I walk
tender heels, coldly exposed.

A year later, he does a load, over
my shyness: discovering all the casual daily traces
of bodily failure. Meeting the ripped underpants,
aging brassieres, stockings laddered at the back
where no one sees. And promptly returns with all folded–
the t-shirts orderly, blouses gently handled, panties
folded with a tenderness
that makes me blush. Socks and bras
tucked in, neatly twinned,
his Army brat inheritance. Yet one blue anklet is left
over: wallflower. And he apologizes, searches the car,
while I laugh, and toss it on the bed. A synthetic snake
has entered our garden. Next night, he brings me
a new pair,
one of his own, to over-pay my loss.
But the lone sock
remains, reminder:
every dresser drawer harbours a few.

Moving in, Together: Personal Effects

along with the boxes, lists and lawyer's bills,
the mortgage mountain atlased
on her shoulders,
and the joint-custody agreement riding his,
they bring with them
the following personal effects:

—one double mattress, delivered,
now endorsed by their joint signature,
nuptials witnessed by new trees
that knock on windows, squirrels
that denounce the burglary,
one sheet, next night, tacked above one window
in ostentatious privacy

—two phones,
one answering machine he declares redundant,
now that his voice is not inside, chained to tape,
with his poems pronounced into her afternoon absence,
furry voice tickling floating dust
with words for the beloved, invented
day by day,
as she arrives in six o'clock exhaustion
kicks off her shoes, drops keys,
hits the button and feels strong wings
lifting her, again

—one son (8) from a previous marriage (his)—12 years, unlearning

—three diplomas (hers)—11 years, unlearning

—her Baba's fur coat, unworn mothballed armour.
Only common squirrel or nuisance raccoon,
she has discovered, to the chagrin
of anti-fur activist
she once was, in the South.

—his Poppy's trapping knife, taken to the island with them in October
and used to cut her clotted shoelaces
after the portage she showed off at, lifting the canoe
for two seconds of elevation, swaying
under its dark wing
before dropping in the mud

—the memory of
daily seven o-clock phone calls
they both breathed, beat towards,
that sewed the days together,
stitched with plans, dinners, worries,
lovetalk and teasing, nags and nicknames,
trying out the edges
of the new island, its marshes and mountains,
that they have cast away on, without lifeboat
but with lists, unfinished manuscripts, baggage

    and this—this knowledge
    that they will fear and falter,
    anxiety rolling in arctic waves under
    blazing moments, sky-climbing.
    Amazed by these
    young innocents, only a month ago,
    signing it all into being, looking over
    their shoulders for the first footprints
    marking the new shore;
    know that they will wake and wonder, eyes wander
    across all the space that owns and invents them,
    try to tie all up in a package, picture, perfect—
    fail

    but know that they will glimpse, at times
    in the other's eyes
    the reflection of a tenderness
    so old, so new
    it almost feels
    like home

lingering bird

—for Ian

Clouds drop
and forests thin. A skin
of ice slows the stream
as the land dreams of snow.
The flight
is on, and wings are tested.
Still he lingers, the great blue
standing at the new edge
of the pool,
amber eye frozen
as we flash past, on track,
shaking the trees to the ground.

and still you linger
migratory companion,
appointments and errands fallen
like feathers
on the bedroom floor–
Nesting in the chill,
warm wings lift,
open
locking down
your heart.

"Scenic Caves"

Photographed on Ontario's summer Mountain,
we look down on Lake Huron,
and long for Blue. Some whimsical elevation
has brought us to these ancient glacial crevices,
chill shadows, holes and traps—my new husband, my stepson
and me. Unsmiling, except at Japanese
tourists who share our lost tongues,
we pay twenty dollars to look at rock—
to climb the cold, hard, slippery ribcage
of this sleeping dinosaur of granite and limestone
unwarmed by August's mellow haze, below.

Ahead of me, the scorning child who won't wait,
neck of the man I won't speak to
as I finger our pamphlet, trying to
match up words with rock, find that happy
tourist "A-ha!", while mosquitoes attack from the fern beds
whining like unanswered questions:
Mesozoic? or Mesolithic?
and which Indian tribe actually used one cranny
for a refrigerator, one cave for council hall, or even
(I read) "a place to ritually debrain
the dead," and "take away all their memories
of earth, so they would lie
peacefully here." The ten-year-old says, "Oooh, gross!"
And scowls as I hand him the camera, then lean back
at Lover's Lookout, our arms half-touching.
I would gladly lie down
for the shaman's bone scalpel, burdened
with pre-framed memories–Georgian Bay
and all its promises
of past and future vacations–going on,
for someone else, smilingly elsewhere.

Joining the line of climbers, neon t-shirts, tourist

shoulder bags, camera lifejackets, the boy races through
each sign-posted challenge—Eagle's Escape,
Printing Press, the Icebox, the Ladder–refuses to stop for
the obligatory snaps that will prove something
weeks away. My husband helps the Japanese grandmother over a boulder,
her gap-toothed smile, bird laugh, and gold pantsuit
entering a non-Kodak moment.
Giggly granddaughters
shake charm bracelets and tiny cameras on thin ovaltine arms
on the way to Fat Man's Misery. "C'mon, let's be
the first ones through," the boy says.
Winding into moss-damp shadow, the man I came with and I
squint at the light-eating crack looming around the corner.
And I know
no matter how slim I am, how photogenic, how brave
I will not enter that darkness, physically,
that we sat in, after breakfast, when he said
"There's no point talking to you, now. Is there."

Ahead the boy slips through with barely a grunt. First smile
of the day. Shouts back, "That was easy!"
The man I came with looks at me, shrugs,
then seeing a fat lady in purple spandex shorts
turning the corner and yelling back "Maury—you gotta try this!"
groans, adjusts his glasses. Descends to a fastidious muttering wriggle
between green-bearded towers
and meets his son on the other side. High-fives, the
congratulatory
click of cameras, beyond my dark lingering
with the smiling, sweating leftovers:
Mrs. Maury and Grandmother and Maury, now panting up the path.
To complete the picture, it follows
that I must   ooze my   yielding bones
stubborn bruised flesh
through the eye of that ancient-smelling needle.
Smell of decay, of fermenting mud
breeding new life, fills my lungs
as I slide stiffly down, backbones meeting.

Then the light
of a foreign flashbulb
catches me, sweaty, moss-stained
and kicking through—
laughing relief,
at the two waiting faces
whose smiles shadow mine,
surprising softening
of stone lips.

divorcing the lake
—on moving off Trout Lake, North Bay

Since we no longer share
the same blue living room,
annul this intimate kinship
of sleeping together, winter to summer–

February, we slid down onto eye-aching plains
–colonized by fishing huts, dog turds, ski-doo trails–
bearing the whine of late night joy-riders testing winter's hold
until somebody's son plunges
into silence. Icy statistics, black and white of newsprint morning
arriving on tomorrow's doorstep.
April, candle ice, wind-driven, roared against the shore
turning the old boathouse, of creosote-coated railway ties,
into *The Titanic*. Walls of gelid water slowly shrank back into
windows
onto July's nakedness, August's gold. Wet dog pacing
the dock, shadow-boxing with the bass teasing beneath
as morning sun marched into noon, then took our deck hostage,
to retreat behind the hill that still houses Cold War radar.

Abandoning this watch
means breaking the binding of our steps
to six seasons of withdrawal and immersion.
Any season, we could step out, nights,
heartbeats hushed by a bigger pulse, the mirroring dark below
which rolled over fish, decayed docks, muskrats, swimmers, dogs,
accommodating the loon's elastic eulogy, evinrude roars
and bushplane takeoffs that, for a second,
split the sky
like ice.

Now we will live as former mates do–
detached, distant, wary of
coming too close. Will not

84

pursue meetings from the other side
despite swelling lament
even the dog wakes to, dry-landed,
for the time when our bodies were harmonized, held by yours,
my babies, floating within a tinier ocean, rocked by cool cradles.
Each time we jumped in,
each time we climbed out: reminding us
of where we have all begun. The muskrat
that patrolled the banks at dusk,
gulls that bobbed, pirate silver,
and every twist of our kitchen tap, gulp of unfiltered trust
as we touched the source–joined with muck, fish and all animals
that live, and die, by the water.

evolution

Hushing in the dark bedroom
after day's detail-hectic flush
on early winter nights, warming
we build this nest
of bone and flesh
above the egg of my belly,
fruitful stories flowering
around a seed inherited
from the future—

knowing our shared breathing
and whispered telling
of what we don't know
is a flame-flicker of magic,
dancing back to chanting cave shadows
and magic roots for holy women to eat

and that all our protections, hopes, blessings
cannot blanket the risk, the crack in the world
we have discovered,
peering down into a chasm
which may hide a volcano, ready to erupt
which may conceal
a Shangri-la, unexplored dimension
where dinosaurs still riot and munch trees
and tiny hunter-gatherers
run from thunder and shadows
of large, flightless birds
shot for cheap meat
before biologists were invented.

We cannot choose
between scientist and frightened ape,
we are our past and our future
and the wonderful terror is

what will succeed us,
in our fully-evolved, failing flesh
our alert, too-often-hurting minds,
cancer-sensitive skin, stretched thin over the cave.
Is evolution still possible? Given ozone depletion, PCBs,
guns in school yards, population explosion, AIDS,
casual divorce and the reflex of war?
Are we, fingers locked in the dark?

Are you, Our You?

THE MOTHER
ROBE

Brooding; Mother's Day Weekend

With no geraniums but two eggs in the flowerbox,
my mother's eighth-floor balcony,
has a bird's eye view, harbouring
a nest. Just a few moultings, dead twigs tumbled,
scratches in the unwatered soil
and the pigeon's will, sitting,
that there IS a nest.
Her neck, indigo rainbow
lengthens as I open the door. She jumps off,
slips behind, huddling against hot metal
marking the end of human mobility,
beginnings of flight. Kneeling
on the concrete, I poke the specked eggs,
smaller than a hen's—warm
to my intruding digit—still surrounded
by crumbs of mocked mothball, the Super's cure.

Then turn back inside, tea with Mom,
as the pigeon resettles,

like that smell in the elevator
nesting between floors,
of old lady's coats and cats and reheated soup.
Neither mothballs nor cats
can stop the balcony occupation
of the mindless mothering birds
who have outlasted Bathurst Street's garbage gulls,
their blinding white wings and *yenta* quarrels.
Instead, the platforms belong to these dowagers
who clatter, flap and coo as dawn pushes under
my mother's sleepmask, inside;
who leave their spatter-paint mess, and nests,
raising up unrepentant eggs.

Twenty minutes later, we decide to step out, claim our share
of sky. The pigeon, half-shadowed, is still her song.
My mother could push the eggs over, to fry on the summer sidewalk,
by *Visitors*. But her hands are dumb, numbed
by those bright gold eyes that watch and do not blink.
She's a good mother, she tells me, sinking into a sprouting lawnchair,
She sits there day, and night. No breaks, no husband. No daycare.
What's a mother to do? My mother's blue-grey eyes
flare in pride, then shamed laughter
cradling the still-warm teacup in her hands:
I'm the only one with a nest;
really, I think the neighbour is jealous.

Standing up, we watch the sun glint off glass of a dozen cars, below,
turning into the garden of granite and marble.
At least once a week,
she tells me, she can watch the mourners come
and go. We clutch the railing and wait.
The flash of car doors, the gathering of family,
flap of a hand, arms half-raised, then lowered
like useless wings. The walk and the pause,
to the new-made place,
the slower walk back.
This ritual seems shrunken by distance

reduced, at eight floors, to some semaphore of instinct.

The pigeon sits under shadows of sharp noon,
and we wait with her:

counting half-completed circles
drawn on the dust.

Penelope in Odyssey

Turning and twisting
in the wine-dark sea
of forty-two weeks' odyssey,
you were dreamed in autumn
out of our daring hope
and surfaced, mid-summer
blown by storming waves
into the wet pre-dawn light
of labour's fifteen-hour triumph
and your mother's wild cry
before your own sailor's announcement
of landfall. Big little woman,
weaving destiny from a web
of tangled blood threads,
You already harbour the seeds
of your own interior ocean.

Long fingers grasp so tiny, so strong
rose mouth reaching out, trusting
for what I did not know was there,
you were welcomed
by wise and brave women,
your mother among them,
and wrapped in the warmth
of your father's arms,
which ached from coaxing
your safe passage home
between the rocky straits of
the uncertainty of birth
to the constantly shifting ground
of a suddenly enlarged earth:

you emptied the nine-months space
under my heart
only to enter it forever.

the art of thumbsucking

this bundle of will and wet diaper, searches
for thumb: blind hand hovering
over shut eyes, craving rose mouth
trying out the fit of fingers and lip
to nest between tongue and still-toothless gum—

and already, you are crawling away
creating your own mother
in self-soothing, wet suckles,
choking back tears and snot-snuffles
as I watch, watch and cradle-rock
you closer to dream—

or the pulsing dark cave
from which you came, carried
in all high-waisted, sentimental labelled
dumb bigness of the breeding female—

little girl, suck in the outside: you mother me
when you find such comfort, simplicity
in what is already to hand.

Poem for September 13th, 2001 *

While the ashes still fell
jumbling DNA dreams:
faith-crazed, headline-effaced
attackers and victims
hanging from the sky....

While the darkness roared
blanketing September gilding
paralysing our vision,
while reasonable men and women
lost television tongues,
returning our eyes again and again to
the fallen towers
bearing fragments of fate
named in the thousands....

And as the rain descended after, drops
crawling for the ocean....

You crashed through, baby woman:
violet-limbed, still trailing the knotted tie,
like a parachute;
piercing the pall with knife-edged cries,
carried to your mother's aching
emptied belly and cut into history.

Survivor's guilt or not,
your wrinkled, furious brow
took nine months to mould,
with each cry a triumph, each angry lifted
fist, pummeling the alien air,
a claim on our hearts.
The fall is made new, and this aging green century
watered by rivers of a returning spring
this September 2001,
carries away tears and fingerprints
as the nurse presses your dyed sole

to the identification form, entering
your name   as others
are finally written in stone services.
Fifteen-minutes-breathing, you
root for the maternal ocean, meeting
sustenance of milk, rising warm
to the surface of my numbed openings.

We are born into loss
as we are opened by love:
"It's a game of inches and seconds," the grey-suited man
draped in the dust of friends, enemies, strangers
tells the hope-hungry world
in the same paper that declares your arrival.
He escaped the fireball down 78 stories
breathing soot and screams and the ceaseless quest
for ground. Ran into the embrace of strangers,
keening of sirens. And found his way home, an unfamiliar
four-miles walk
out of yesterday.

And as you are born into tomorrow
this season of loss and uncovering
suddenly we are rooted to the same page;
sharing both beginning and ending
in the tenacious grip of a tiny hand,
like my heart, pulsing
hope and despair–
like the foreign grip on familiar controls
which may bring us back to
earth, together
if only to be claimed by its gravity.

Second daughter, this day you fly
the present forever into the past
astonishing, terrifying, marking us
for this moment, a lifetime's
opening.

   *two days after the terrorist attacks in America.

———
94

Time Coming

–for Helen Kowalchuk (1904-2005) U.S.S.R.-Canada

I

For thirty-five years,
"Time coming," Baba used to mutter. Satisfaction
in the argument-ending certainty
of a clock hand's crawl, moving her out in the company
of ancestors, saints and the pre-ordered funeral package, planting
her beside husband #2, Emilyan, who fell from her pruning.
Satisfaction, in the way she wrung a dishcloth
or stabbed at the potatoes. Comfort in the silence she could
generate, dark cloud spreading like squid's ink as we sat at her
table, forking down
mountains of cabbage, beef and rice,
pickled beets bleeding
onto chipped Woolco saucers. "Not gonna live forever–"
 Though every year
we denied it–grew up, older–and she disproved it. Seventy-five,
eighty, ninety and beyond. To the Nursing Home, where they
only spoke English. Hired illegal immigrants
to wash, dress and wheel our grandparents, weekly deposits
at the Visitor's Room.

II

At 100, she descends to a wheelchair, without benefit of an MP's
photo-opp. Celebrations turn to accusations of her seventy-eight-
year old son, now known as her brother, and "stealing my new
potatoes–thief!" No longer Miss Clairol-orange, her feathers of white
fire wildly as she fixes me, the unexpected Wedding Guest, Christmas,
with an eye ever-bright for the world's worry. It's the boys, she tells
us, a river of words, in Russian, then English, they need shelter, and
clothes. "Police, lost, lost. Poor *Chupchik**." Who will help? Her
flood won't be dammed by barriers erected feebly now, with
comments on the weather, a gift of soap, the plastic evergreen.

"Ah, the winters were terrible there", whether Kirkland Lake or her village in Belarus. "Yes, Nicky, he was going to become a teacher, but he needed new shoes. And a pair of glasses—he broke the last ones, chased home from school by that bully, Anton." I sit up; Dad sighs. "You know, I rang and rang, I was trying to phone the police, but *that woman*, she never came." A nurse passes, peers in and says isn't it nice that Grandma has visitors for Christmas. And that it's almost lunch time. Baba glares, "And the soup, I wanted to tell you, it had no flavour at all. A nothing soup."

III

Diapers called Depends are now changed by brisk brown women who know her as Elly, always talking about her washing or cooking. Cutting down her skirts and blouses to clothe the lost boys, so that she sits in Walmart sacks, tattered and safety-pinned. Now in Russia, now in Kirkland where husband #1, Mike, finally brought her and *chupchik,* Baba rides the halls of memory, startling the blank faces she meets. In conversation with her "brother" who remembers her son's birth. She, 21, in a shed beside the wheatfield she was scything. Two women watching. "I was so thin, so young. Had no milk. Had to hand him to the woman beside me, her baby died. Anton."

Stopping before the photos of her 100th birthday party, she jabs a finger and says "See, my mother–like monkey–she lived too long, too long–"

IV

As we listen, her second granddaughter, 39, waits in hospital for the pains, the driving division that will turn her world inside out, begun again. Her husband holding her hand, rubbing her back, drinking her fear but ready with the camera and the rose in plastic. The ghost that haunted her nine-month house of flesh will put his feet down, sensing earth, now hidden under the first snow. Claim flesh's dear indignities, and a name. The purple wail that ends with him crushed to her filling breast, an echo down the halls of memory

of the hundred years of his great-grandmother's losing, gaining
and worrying.
The mother, the timekeeper. Like the puppy trick:
a hot water bottle and clock, wrapped in flannel,
tucked beside the whimpering whelp
whose only comfort is breathing in the beats
of mother time.

* "child" (Russian)

With the Soccer Parents

On this wet-sponge August day,
half the town is under twelve, and playing soccer. Tournament time
ambers us
in a moment of ancient struggle
for victory, vindication or a good cry, on the drive home.
A carnival sheen greases the grass, like the promise of rain.
Balloon-curling clowns
nametagged "Sparky" or "Bubbles"
menace little sisters with sausage dogs or daisies,
real dogs patrol the BBQ table, sensing butterfly stomachs,
while on the field, four-year-olds trip over their jerseys, swarming
like gulls after fries.
Parents, raising camcorders, order charging players to "Look at Dad!
Look at Dad!" while another helps the goalie release her ribboned
braids, caught in the netting,
like a moth, trapped in the windowscreen, between worlds.

Co-workers, cops, counselors, bank managers and more
parents all, publicly-revealed, complicit in this ritual of winning, we know:
meeting with a nervous nod, weary smile, tugged-at hand
in the lineups for hotdogs, toilets, team medals.
We are the shamefaced-proud lawnchair audience
of goal drivers and cloud-watchers alike,
teeth clenching when she slips on the goalie jersey
or he puts the ball in, audaciously, at his own end.
Between games, we meet each other again, rewrite the victories, ties,
losses of nine to none,
selfishly, as our own. Popped balloons and dropped dogs,
these games resuscitate our own six- and seven-year-old bodies,
shadowing the playing fields, the backyards, the camps, the gyms.
We are the kids puddled with tears at a lost balloon
or a lost game, a missed promotion, a slipped
disk, a separation agreement. And barely nod,
as we meet each other's eyes, measuring confidence like tans
under the sagging tent where medals are awarded,

by coaches hoarsely proud or resigned—teachers, uncles, waitresses,
girl guide leaders, ourselves—calling in their players, like lost sheep
(or souls),
to touch each sticky palm, hang over each thin neck
the one-size-fits-all medal,
courtesy of *Horton's,* that they will
gloat over, sleep in, drape over their bedposts
to be stolen again and again by little sisters and finally, lost on the first day
of school. As summer ends with a cloudburst,
parents' eyes prickle—
Non-losers, every one.

comforting the child in the dark

at three and a half/in shadow
she begs me "to watch" until she falls asleep
beneath the black hole ruling her bedtime hour:
white ceiling light half-gleaming, half-face-cratered;
silver Man-in-the-Moon grin
ready to reach down, swallow up this traveller, whole–

already, she is marking distance, grieving
even loss of scribbled pages, toothpaste tubes and gluesticks
she embraced to sticky excess–
"I hate that things have to go away," she says,
consumed companions tossed too quickly in the trash.

I hate it too,
hate the arrival of shadow
in her formerly star-glowing nursery
our hand-painted ceiling torn away to reveal
a leaking plaster face,
which the man standing on the silver ladder erased
so torn ribbons of yellow stars/blue sky
came down to earth, dropped into the dumpster.

Now she looks up into a vacant face, blank page printed
by imagination and the cold hands of nightmare
creeping up the back of a neck, shaking you awake–
as my husband was last night, muttering
about a hovering bird, the dark–
to mutter and shake quietly in my arms

she says
"I miss my ceiling. And I miss my crib."

with nightlights and a squadron of stuffed animals
we fight the dark for her
stories with princess endings

and just one more "tight hug". Can't tell her, in words
all the faith I have on this earth
is found in her cloudless questioning: "Where do people go,
when they die?"

already, she knows that flowers fold back into earth
consumed by an insect underground
spilling from our compost pile to elicit her screams and stomps;
that hearts stop, sometime somewhere for someone,
that missing grandmothers must be sought in bedtime whispers, quick kisses,
somewhere beside
un-painted stars and empty-mouthed moon,
beside ghosts of her lonely father and me, one month to go:
he holding the wooden ladder, my legs
for my doubled unsteadiness
while I reached up, with yellow paint, for her:

placing our path
out of the dark.

About the Author

Laurie Kruk published her first book of poetry, *Theories of the World*, in 1992, the same year she received her doctorate from the University of Western Ontario. After enjoying a postdoctoral year of study in Vancouver, she was lured to Northern Ontario, to teach English at newly-independent Nipissing University of North Bay. There her adventures expanded to include marriage, a dog, a sojourn on Trout Lake, camping, two daughters and a step-son. Since her early days of feeling like an "alien," she has grown to love "the near North"—its dramatic landscapes, resilient inhabitants and strong sense of community. Specializing in Canadian Literature, Kruk is also the author of *The Voice is the Story: Conversations with Canadian Writers of Short Fiction* (2003).